D0365659

MAHS

SHRIEKS AT MIDNIGHT

SHRIEKS
AT MIDNIGHT

Macabre Poems, Eerie and Humorous

Selected by Sara and John E. Brewton

DRAWINGS BY ELLEN RASKIN

Thomas Y. Crowell Company   New York

Copyright © 1969 by Sara and John E. Brewton
Illustrations copyright © 1969 by Ellen Raskin

All rights reserved. Except for use in a review, the reproduction
or utilization of this work in any form or by any electronic,
mechanical, or other means, now known or hereafter invented,
including xerography, photocopying, and recording, and in
any information storage and retrieval system is forbidden
without the written permission of the publisher.
Designed by Ellen Raskin
Manufactured in the United States of America

L. C. Card 69-11824

ISBN: 0-690-73518-9

5 6 7 8 9 10

*Grateful acknowledgment is made to the following authors,
publishers, and other copyright holders for permission to
reprint copyrighted material.*

ABELARD-SCHUMAN LIMITED for "The Cat!" by Joseph Payne Brennan from *Halloween Through Twenty Centuries* compiled by Ralph
and Adelin Linton, copyright 1950 by Henry Schuman, Inc.

EDWARD ARNOLD (PUBLISHERS) LTD. for "The Bath" from *The
Motley Muse* by Harry Graham and "Quiet Fun" from *More Ruthless Rhymes* by Harry Graham.

MORRIS BISHOP for his poem "A Ghoulish Old Fellow in Kent,"
first published in *The New Yorker*, copyright © 1954 by Morris
Bishop.

OLIVE W. BURT for one stanza of "Lydia Sherman" from *American
Murder Ballads and Their Stories* collected by Olive W. Burt, published by Oxford University Press.

CALDER AND BOYARS, LTD., for four lines from "After Lorca" from
Poems 1950-1965 by Robert Creeley, copyright 1966 by Calder and
Boyars, Ltd.

NATHALIA CRANE for "Spooks" from *The Singing Crow and Other Poems* by Nathalia Crane, published by Albert and Charles Boni, Inc.

CRESCENDO PUBLISHERS for "The Two Wives" from *Frontiers* by Daniel Henderson, copyright 1933, published by Bruce Humphries, Inc., reprinted by permission of Crescendo Publishers, Boston.

CURTIS BROWN, LTD., for "A Second Stanza for Dr. Johnson" from *Exiles & Marriages* by Donald Hall, copyright © 1954 by Donald Hall, published by the Viking Press; "There Was an Old Lady Named Crockett" from *Typewriter Town* by William Jay Smith, copyright © 1960 by William Jay Smith, published by E. P. Dutton & Co., Inc.

PAUL DEHN for his poems "In a Cavern," first printed in *Punch*, and "Miss Muffet," from *Quake, Quake, Quake* by Paul Dehn, published by Simon & Schuster, Inc.

DODD, MEAD & COMPANY, INC., for "The Cremation of Sam McGee" by Robert W. Service from *The Complete Poems of Robert Service*, copyright 1940 by Robert Service, with the permission also of ERNEST BENN LIMITED and THE RYERSON PRESS; "The Rhyme of the Chivalrous Shark" from *Nautical Lays of a Landsman* by Wallace Irwin.

DOUBLEDAY & COMPANY, INC., for "Johnny" by Emma Rounds from *Creative Youth* edited by Hughes Mearns, copyright 1925 by Doubleday & Company, Inc.; for "Epitaph for a Postal Clerk," copyright © 1956 by X. J. Kennedy, from *Nude Descending a Staircase,* copyright © 1961 by X. J. Kennedy, with the permission also of CURTIS BROWN, LTD. (This poem originally appeared in *The New Yorker*.)

E. P. DUTTON & CO., INC., for "Hell's Bells," copyright 1932, 1937 by E. P. Dutton & Co., Inc., renewal, ©, 1960, 1965 by Margaret Fishback Antolini, from the book *One to a Customer* by Margaret Fishback; "My Singing Aunt" and "The Old Wife and the Ghost" from the book *The Blackbird in the Lilac* by James Reeves, published 1959 by E. P. Dutton & Co., Inc., 1952 by Oxford University Press, with the permission also of OXFORD UNIVERSITY PRESS; "The Two Old Women of Mumbling Hill" and "You'd Think It Was a Funeral" from the book *The Wandering Moon* by James Reeves, published 1960 by E. P. Dutton & Co., Inc., with the permission also of William Heinemann Ltd.; "The Flattered Flying Fish" from the book *The Flattered Flying Fish and Other Poems* by E. V. Rieu, copyright,

© 1962 by E. V. Rieu, with the permission also of METHUEN & COMPANY LTD.

PAUL ELDRIDGE for his poem "Wang Peng's Recommendation for Improving the People."

THE FURROW for "Clock Time by the Geyser" by John White, from the March-April 1964 issue of *The Furrow*, copyright 1964.

MRS. ARTHUR GUITERMAN for "The Superstitious Ghost" from *The Mirthful Lyre* by Arthur Guiterman, copyright 1918 by Harper and Brothers.

HARPER & ROW, PUBLISHERS, for "For a Lady I Know," "For a Mouthy Woman," and "For a Pessimist" from *On These I Stand* by Countee Cullen, copyright 1925 by Harper & Row, Publishers, renewed 1953 by Ida M. Cullen.

SAMUEL HOFFENSTEIN for "Madrigal Macabre" and two stanzas of "Song, On Reading That the Cyclotron Has Produced Cosmic Rays" from *Pencil in the Air* by Samuel Hoffenstein, copyright 1947 by Samuel Hoffenstein, published by Doubleday & Company, Inc.

ETHEL JACOBSON for her poems "Atomic Courtesy" and "Lines Scratched in Wet Cement," which was first printed in *Look* magazine, copyright 1965.

W. LOWRIE KAY for his poem "Lancaster County Tragedy," first printed in the *Atlantic Monthly*, March 1967, copyright 1967.

MRS. STODDARD KING for the poem "Commissary Report" by Stoddard King.

ALFRED A. KNOPF, INC., and A. D. PETERS & CO. for "B Stands for Bear" (ten lines from "A Moral Alphabet"), "Jim Who Ran Away from His Nurse," "Henry King Who Chewed Bits of String," and "The Python" from *Cautionary Verses* by Hilaire Belloc, published 1939 by Gerald Duckworth Ltd and 1941 by Alfred A. Knopf, Inc.

MARTIN LEVIN for "Epitaph" by Leslie Mellichamp from Martin Levin's "Phoenix Nest," *Saturday Review*, September 19, 1959; "Donne Redone" by Joseph Paul Tierney from Martin Levin's "Phoenix Nest," *Saturday Review*, August 8, 1964.

MRS. NEWMAN LEVY for "The Revolving Door" from *Gay but Wistful* by Newman Levy, copyright 1925 by Newman Levy, published by Alfred A. Knopf, Inc.

J. B. LIPPINCOTT COMPANY for one stanza of "Please, Johnny" from *The Man Who Sang the Sillies* by John Ciardi, copyright © 1961 by John Ciardi. "Epitaph for Any New Yorker" from *Parsons' Pleasure* by Christopher Morley, copyright 1923 by George H. Doran Company, copyright renewed 1951 by Christopher Morley; "Epitaph on the Proofreader of the Encyclopedia Britannica" from *The Rocking Horse* by Christopher Morley, copyright 1919, 1947 by Christopher Morley; "Thoughts for St. Stephen" from *Mandarin in Manhattan* by Christopher Morley, copyright 1933 by Christopher Morley, copyright renewed © 1961 by Mrs. Helen Morley.

LITTLE, BROWN AND COMPANY for "Any Day Now" from *Odds Without Ends* by David McCord, copyright 1954 by David McCord; "The Purist," copyright 1935 by The Curtis Publishing Company, "The Termite," copyright 1942 by The Curtis Publishing Company, "Lucy Lake," originally published in *The New Yorker*, copyright 1933 by Ogden Nash, and "The Lion," copyright 1944 by The Curtis Publishing Company, from *Verses from 1929 On* by Ogden Nash, and for ten lines from "Adventures of Isabel," copyright 1936 by Ogden Nash, from *Many Long Years Ago* by Ogden Nash, with the permission also of J. M. Dent & Sons Ltd, publishers of *Family Reunion* and *Good Intentions* by Ogden Nash; "The Monkeys and the Crocodile" by Laura E. Richards.

THE MACMILLAN COMPANY for "Brother and Sister" from *Useful and Instructive Poetry* by Lewis Carroll, copyright 1954 by Frances Menella Dodgson, with the permission also of the EXECUTORS OF THE ESTATE OF THE LATE LEWIS CARROLL; "The Great Auk's Ghost" from *Poems* by Ralph Hodgson, copyright 1945, with the permission also of GEORGE ALLEN & UNWIN LTD, publishers of *The Last Blackbird* by Ralph Hodgson; "The Lion" from *Johnny Appleseed and Other Poems* by Vachel Lindsay, copyright 1913, 1914, 1917, 1925, and 1928; "Little Boys of Texas" from *Collected Poems of Robert P. Tristram Coffin*, copyright 1945.

MEREDITH PRESS for "St. Swithin" from *Harp in the Winds* by Daniel Henderson, copyright, 1924, by D. Appleton and Company.

HAROLD OBER ASSOCIATES INC. for "Request for Requiems" from *One Way Ticket* by Langston Hughes, copyright 1948 by Alfred A. Knopf, Inc.; "Wake" from *Shakespeare in Harlem* by Langston Hughes, copyright 1942 by Alfred A. Knopf, Inc.

A. D. PETERS & COMPANY for "On a Politician" from *Sonnets and Verse* by Hilaire Belloc, published by Gerald Duckworth Ltd.

SYDNEY KING RUSSELL for "Dust" from *Selected Poems* by Sydney King Russell, copyright 1949 by Sydney King Russell, published by House of Falmouth, Inc.

CHARLES SCRIBNER'S SONS for four lines from "After Lorca" from *For Love,* copyright © 1962 by Robert Creeley; "Away with Bloodshed" and "Hallelujah" by A. E. Housman from *My Brother, A. E. Housman,* copyright 1937, 1938 by Laurence Housman, copyright 1937, 1938 by Laurence Housman, renewal copyright © 1965, 1966 by Lloyds Bank Limited, with the permission also of THE SOCIETY OF AUTHORS as the literary representative of the Estate of the late A. E. Housman, and MESSRS. JONATHAN CAPE LTD., publishers of A. E. Housman's *Collected Poems.*

SIMON & SCHUSTER, INC., for "The Hydrogen Dog and the Cobalt Cat" by Frederick Winsor from *The Space Child's Mother Goose* by Frederick Winsor and Marion Parry, copyright © 1956, 1957, 1958 by Frederick Winsor and Marion Parry.

THE SOCIETY OF AUTHORS for "Bones," "The Eel," and "Ponjoo" by Walter de la Mare from *Stuff and Nonsense,* reprinted by permission of the Literary Trustees of Walter de la Mare and The Society of Authors as their representative.

DOROTHY BROWN THOMPSON for the lines from her poem "Fe-Fi-Fo-Fum," copyright 1934 by Dorothy Brown Thompson, first printed in *St. Nicholas* magazine, August 1934.

TODAY'S HEALTH, published by the American Medical Association, for the poems "Epitaph" by Richard Armour and "Primer of Consequences" by Virginia Brasier, published in *Today's Health,* January 1953, copyright 1953.

THE VIKING PRESS, INC., for "The Crusader" from "Tombstones in the Starlight" by Dorothy Parker, which originally appeared in *The New Yorker,* from *The Portable Dorothy Parker,* copyright 1929, copyright © renewed 1957 by Dorothy Parker; "Résumé" by Dorothy Parker from *The Portable Dorothy Parker,* copyright 1926, renewed 1954 by Dorothy Parker.

EUPHEMIA ANN WOLFE for the lines translated by Humbert Wolfe from *The Greek Anthology,* first published under the title "The Quack" from *Others Abide* by Humbert Wolfe.

Books Compiled by John E. Brewton

UNDER THE TENT OF THE SKY

GAILY WE PARADE

POETRY TIME

With Sara Brewton:

CHRISTMAS BELLS ARE RINGING

BRIDLED WITH RAINBOWS

SING A SONG OF SEASONS

BIRTHDAY CANDLES BURNING BRIGHT

LAUGHABLE LIMERICKS

AMERICA FOREVER NEW
A Book of Poems

SHRIEKS AT MIDNIGHT
Macabre Poems, Eerie and Humorous

INDEX TO CHILDREN'S POETRY

INDEX TO CHILDREN'S POETRY
First Supplement

INDEX TO CHILDREN'S POETRY
Second Supplement

Contents

The poems in this book are about death and doom, ghosts and ghouls, bare bones and shiverous beasts. Ghoulish and grim, eerie and shivery—with a whiff of murder, death, and doom—these macabre verses also have a touch of humor—*grave* humor.

> . . . shrieks at midnight
> And steps of thunder—
> And I inch up closer
> Under the lamp. . . .
>   —*Dorothy Brown Thompson*

Shrieks at Midnight

I do like ogres——
There's something about them
So utterly ruthless
And yet absurd!
      I don't believe in them,
Yet I shiver
The very instant
I hear the word——
FE—FI—FO——*FUM!*

—DOROTHY BROWN THOMPSON

from AN OLD CORNISH LITANY

From Ghoulies and Ghosties,
And long-leggity Beasties,
And all things that go bump in the night,
Good Lord deliver us.

—Author Unknown

THE GREAT AUK'S GHOST

The Great Auk's ghost rose on one leg,
Sighed thrice and three times winkt,
And turned and poached a phantom egg
And muttered, "I'm extinct."

—Ralph Hodgson

A SKELETON ONCE IN KHARTOUM

A skeleton once in Khartoum
Asked a spirit up into his room;
    They spent the whole night
    In the eeriest fight
As to which should be frightened of whom.

—Author Unknown

SPOOKS

Oh, I went down to Framingham
   To sit on a graveyard wall;
"If there be spooks," I said to myself,
   "I shall see them, one and all."

I hugged the knee to still the heart,
   My gaze on a tomb 'neath a tree.
Down in the village the clock struck nine,
   But never a ghost did I see.

A boy passed by, and his hair was red;
   He paused by a sunken mound.
"How goes it with all the ghosts?" said he.
   "Have you heard any walking around?"

Now the taunt was the sign of a boy's disdain
    For the study I did pursue.
So I took the hour to teach that lad
    Of the things unseen but true.

And suddenly a bat swung by,
    Two cats began to bawl,
And that red-haired boy walked off in haste
    When I needed him most of all.

I lost a slipper as I fled—
    I bumped against a post;
But nevertheless I knew I'd won
    The secret of raising a ghost.

And the method is this—at least for a miss—
    You must sit on a graveyard wall,
And talk of the things you never have seen,
    And you'll see them, one and all.

                    —*Nathalia Crane*

THE GHOST THAT JIM SAW

Why, as to that, said the engineer,
Ghosts ain't things we are apt to fear;
Spirits don't fool with levers much,
And throttle-valves don't take to such;
    And as for Jim,
    What happened to him
Was one half fact, and t'other half whim!

Running one night on the line, he saw
A house—as plain as the moral law—
Just by the moonlit bank, and thence
Came a drunken man with no more sense
    Than to drop on the rail
    Flat as a flail,
As Jim drove by with the midnight mail.

Down went the patents—steam reversed.
Too late! for there came a "thud." Jim cursed
As the fireman, there in the cab with him,
Kinder stared in the face of Jim,
    And says, "What now?"
    Says Jim, "What now!
I've just run over a man,—that's how!"

The fireman stared at Jim. They ran
Back, but they never found house nor man,—
Nary a shadow within a mile.

Jim turned pale, but he tried to smile,
    Then on he tore
    Ten mile or more,
In quicker time than he'd made afore.

Would you believe it! the very next night
Up rose that house in the moonlight white,
Out comes the chap and drops as before,
Down goes the brake and the rest encore;
    And so, in fact,
    Each night that act
Occurred, till folks swore Jim was cracked.

Humph! let me see; it's a year now, 'most,
That I met Jim, East, and says, "How's your ghost?"
"Gone," says Jim; "and more, it's plain
That ghost don't trouble me again.
    I thought I shook
    That ghost when I took
A place on an Eastern line,—but look!

"What should I meet, the first trip out,
But the very house we talked about,
And the selfsame man! 'Well,' says I, 'I guess
It's time to stop this 'yer foolishness.'
    So I crammed on steam,
    When there came a scream
From my fireman, that jest broke my dream:

" 'You've killed somebody!' Says I, 'Not much!
I've been thar often, and thar ain't no such,
And now I'll prove it!' Back we ran,
And—darn my skin!—but thar *was* a man
    On the rail, dead,
    Smashed in the head!—
Now I call that meanness!" That's all Jim said.

        —Bret Harte

THE SUPERSTITIOUS GHOST

I'm such a quiet little ghost,
  Demure and inoffensive,
The other spirits say I'm most
  Absurdly apprehensive.

Through all the merry hours of night
  I'm uniformly cheerful;
I love the dark; but in the light,
  I own I'm rather fearful.

Each dawn I cower down in bed,
  In every brightness seeing,
That weird uncanny form of dread—
  An awful Human Being!

Of course I'm told they can't exist,
    That Nature would not let them:
But Willy Spook, the Humanist,
    Declares that he has met them!

He says they do not glide like us,
    But walk in eerie paces;
They're solid, not diaphanous,
    With arms! and legs! ! and faces! ! !

And some are beggars, some are kings,
    Some have and some are wanting,
They squander time in doing things,
    Instead of simply haunting.

They talk of "art," the horrid crew,
    And things they call "ambitions."—
Oh, yes, I know as well as you
    They're only superstitions.

But should the dreadful day arrive
    When, starting up, I see one,
I'm sure 'twill scare me quite alive;
    And then—Oh, then I'll be one!

                    —*Arthur Guiterman*

SIR RODERIC'S SONG

When the night wind howls in the chimney cowls, and
    the bat in the moonlight flies,
And inky clouds, like funeral shrouds, sail over the
    midnight skies—
When the footpads quail at the night-bird's wail, and
    black dogs bay the moon,
Then is the spectres' holiday—then is the ghosts' high-
    noon!

As the sob of the breeze sweeps over the trees, and the
    mists lie low on the fen,
From grey tombstones are gathered the bones that once
    were women and men,
And away they go, with a mop and a mow, to the revel
    that ends too soon,
For cockcrow limits our holiday—the dead of the
    night's high-noon!

And then each ghost with his ladye-toast to their
    churchyard beds take flight,
With a kiss, perhaps, on her lantern chaps, and a grisly
    grim "goodnight";
Till the welcome knell of the midnight bell rings forth
    its jolliest tune,
And ushers our next high holiday—the dead of the
    night's high-noon!

—*William Schwenck Gilbert*

THE CAT!

Who pads through the wood
     Where cypresses grow,
When the sun goes down
     And night-winds blow?
     The cat!

Who slinks through the cave
     In the side of the hill
Where black bats swoop
     From a cobwebbed sill?
     The cat!

Who purrs by the grave
     Of unshriven dead,
While witches dance
     And ghouls are fed?
     The cat!... SKAT!!!

—Joseph Payne Brennan

THE TWO WIVES
A New England Legend

Jonathan Moulton lost his wife—
Neighbors said he took her life.
Did he poison or strangle or smother?
Howsoever, he married another.
A shy and unsuspicious thing,
She wore his first wife's wedding ring.

Asleep she lay where the first wife's head
Had pillowed itself on the fateful bed,
But she woke at midnight shivering:
A cold hand plucked at her marriage ring,
And a voice at her ear had a graveyard tone:
"Give the dead her own!"

Jonathan woke at his young bride's scream.
Up he sprang and brought in candles,
But ghostly wives have elfin sandals.
He swore to his bride it was just a dream,
He lifted her hand in the candle gleam.
"I'll wager my all that it's still on."
But—Lord ha'e mercy!—the ring was gone!

—Daniel Henderson

THE TWO OLD WOMEN OF
MUMBLING HILL

The two old trees on Mumbling Hill,
They whisper and chatter and never keep still.
What do they say as they lean together
In rain or sunshine or windy weather?

There were two old women lived near the hill,
And they used to gossip as women will
Of friends and neighbours, houses and shops,
Weather and trouble and clothes and crops.

And one sad winter they both took ill,
The two old women of Mumbling Hill.
They were bent and feeble and wasted away
And both of them died on the selfsame day.

Now the ghosts of the women of Mumbling Hill,
They started to call out loud and shrill,
'Where are the tales we used to tell,
And where is the talking we loved so well?'

Side by side stood the ghosts until
They both took root on Mumbling Hill;
And they turned to trees, and they slowly grew,
Summer and winter the long years through.

In winter the bare boughs creaked and cried,
In summer the green leaves whispered and sighed;
And still they talk of fine and rain,
Storm and sunshine, comfort and pain.

The two old trees of Mumbling Hill,
They whisper and chatter and never keep still.
What do they say as they lean together
In rain or sunshine or windy weather?

—*James Reeves*

MY SINGING AUNT

The voice of magic melody
    With which my aunt delights me,
It drove my uncle to the grave
    And now his ghost affrights me.
This was the song she used to sing
    When I could scarcely prattle,
And as her top notes rose and fell
    They made the sideboard rattle:

'What makes a lady's cheeks so red,
    Her hair both long and wavy?
'Tis eating up her crusts of bread,
    Likewise her greens and gravy.

What makes the sailor tough and gay?
    What makes the ploughboy whistle?
'Tis eating salt-beef twice a day,
    And never mind the gristle.'

Thus sang my aunt in days gone by
    To soothe, caress, and calm me;
But what delighted me so much
    Drove her poor husband barmy.
So now when past the church I stray,
    'Tis not the night-wind moaning,
That chills my blood and stops my breath,
    But poor old uncle's groaning.

—*James Reeves*

THE OLD WIFE AND THE GHOST

There was an old wife and she lived all alone
    In a cottage not far from Hitchin:
And one bright night, by the full moon light,
    Comes a ghost right into her kitchen.

About that kitchen neat and clean
    The ghost goes pottering round.
But the poor old wife is deaf as a boot
    And so hears never a sound.

The ghost blows up the kitchen fire,
    As bold as bold can be;
He helps himself from the larder shelf,
    But never a sound hears she.

He blows on his hands to make them warm,
    And whistles aloud 'Whee-hee!'
But still as a sack the old soul lies
    And never a sound hears she.

From corner to corner he runs about,
    And into the cupboard he peeps;
He rattles the door and bumps on the floor,
    But still the old wife sleeps.

Jangle and bang go the pots and pans,
  As he throws them all around;
And the plates and mugs and dishes and jugs,
  He flings them all to the ground.

Madly the ghost tears up and down
  And screams like a storm at sea;
And at last the old wife stirs in her bed—
  And it's 'Drat those mice,' says she.

Then the first cock crows and morning shows
  And the troublesome ghost's away.
But oh! what a pickle the poor wife sees
  When she gets up next day.

'Them's tidy big mice,' the old wife thinks,
  And off she goes to Hitchin,
And a tidy big cat she fetches back
  To keep the mice from her kitchen.

                    —*James Reeves*

A Whiff of Murder

As he enters the house,
A whiff of murder—
—AUTHOR UNKNOWN

FE, FI, FO, FUM . . .

Fe, fi, fo, fum,
I smell the blood of an Englishman!
Be he alive or be he dead,
I'll grind his bones to make my bread!

—Author Unknown

CASSIE O'LANG

Here lies the body of Cassie O'Lang!
She tried to kill her husband with a boomerang.

—Judge

EPITAPH

Here he lies moulding;
    His dying was hard—
They shot him for folding
    An IBM card.

—Leslie Mellichamp

THE DUEL

Schott and Willing did engage
 In duel fierce and hot;
Schott shot Willing willingly,
 And Willing he shot Schott.

The shot Schott shot made Willing quite
 A spectacle to see;
While Willing's willing shot went right
 Through Schott's anatomy.

—Author Unknown

LATE LAST NIGHT

Late last night I slew my wife,
Stretched her on the parquet flooring:
I was loath to take her life,
But I had to stop her snoring.

—Author Unknown

LINES SCRATCHED IN WET CEMENT

A guest for whom I did not care
 had an utterly uncanny flair
For dropping by my modest lair
When I hadn't swept, but was
 tinting my hair.
She'd finger dust, and with gimlet glare
Pounce upon my shabbiest chair
To chirp with a social-worker air,
"How quaint!"
I took her down to see the cellar,
And nobody knows what there befell her.

—Ethel Jacobson

A GHOULISH OLD FELLOW IN KENT

A ghoulish old fellow in Kent
Encrusted his wife in cement;
 He said, with a sneer:
 "I was careful, my dear,
To follow your natural bent."

—Morris Bishop

LYDIA SHERMAN

Lydia Sherman is plagued with rats.
Lydia has no faith in cats.
So Lydia buys some arsenic,
And then her husband he gets sick;
And then her husband, he does die,
And Lydia's neighbors wonder why.

—Author Unknown

QUIET FUN

My son Augustus, in the street, one day,
   Was feeling quite exceptionally merry.
A stranger asked him: "Can you show me, pray,
   The quickest way to Brompton Cemetery?"
"The quickest way? You bet I can!" says Gus,
   And pushed the fellow underneath a bus.

Whatever people say about my son,
He does enjoy his little bit of fun.

—Harry Graham

LUCY LAKE

Lawsamassy, for heaven's sake!
Have you never heard of Lucy Lake?
Lucy is fluffy and fair and cosy
Lucy is like a budding posy.
Lucy speaks with a tiny lisp,
Lucy's mind is a will-o'-the-wisp.
Lucy is just as meek as a mouse,
Lucy lives in a darling house,
With a darling garden and a darling fence,
And a darling faith in the future tense.
A load of hay, or a crescent moon,
And she knows that things will be better soon.
Lucy resigns herself to sorrow
In building character for tomorrow.
Lucy tells us to carry on,
It's always darkest before the dawn.
A visit to Lucy's bucks you up,
Helps you swallow the bitterest cup.
Lucy Lake is meek as a mouse.
Let's go over to Lucy's house,
And let's lynch Lucy!

—*Ogden Nash*

A SECOND STANZA FOR DR. JOHNSON[1]

I put my hat upon my head
And walk'd into the Strand;
And there I met another man
Whose hat was in his hand.

The only trouble with the man
Whom I had met was that,
As he walked swinging both his arms,
His head was in his hat.

—*Donald Hall*

[1]The first stanza is by Dr. Johnson.

A BRITON WHO SHOT AT HIS KING

A Briton who shot at his king
Was doomed on the gallows to swing.
    When the rope was made fast
    He cried out, "At last!
I'm getting the hang of the thing!"

—*David Ross*

ONE GOOD TURN DESERVES ANOTHER

A poor man went to hang himself,
 But treasure chanced to find:
He pocketed the miser's pelf
 And left the rope behind.

His money gone, the miser hung
 Himself in sheer despair:
Thus each the other's wants supplied,
 And that was surely fair.

     —*Punch* (1841)

RÉSUMÉ

Razors pain you;
Rivers are damp;
Acids stain you;
And drugs cause cramp.
Guns aren't lawful;
Nooses give;
Gas smells awful;
You might as well live.

    —*Dorothy Parker*

ON BELL-RINGERS

Ye rascals of ringers, ye merciless foes,
And disturbers of all who are fond of repose,
How I wish, for the quiet and peace of the land,
That ye wore round your necks what you hold in your
      hand!

—From the French of Voltaire

THE SALVATION OF TEXAS PETERS

We were hangin' "Rustler" Murphy for
      the stealin' of a horse:
It was in the cattle country, where the' was
      no law but force,
An' we had no courts an' lawyers t' steer
      justice fr'm its course.

We were hangin' Rustler Murphy just as
      dawn was showin' dim
In the eastern sky; we had n't nothin' per-
      sonal 'g'in' him,
But a rustler takes his chances, an' his
      chance is mighty slim.

In the hills we heard a coyote sound his
    melancholy wail,
Like a dirge for Rustler Murphy as we led
    him from the jail,
Both his legs amazin' stiddy, though his face
    a little pale.

He was game, was Rustler Murphy, for he
    never said a word
As we marched him up the valley, where
    the long grass waved an' stirred,
An' the music of the coyotes was the only
    sound we heard.

We were hangin' Rustler Murphy just as
    genteel as we could,
For we had n't nothin' personal 'g'in' him
    or his brood,
An' he walked along, resigned-like, just as
    if he understood.

There's a pine-tree up the mountain, where
    we were a-leadin' him—
A tree that once was blasted by the lightnin',
    an' stood grim,
With a black an' shriveled body, but a most
    invitin' limb.

It was handy to the village, an' was fer
enough away,
So the hangin' wa'n't offensive; an' the
dawn was gettin' gray
As we halted our procession, so's to give
him time to pray.

Then up spoke Buckskin Davis, who was
holdin' of the rope
When the rustler's prayer was finished, an'
he hazarded a hope
That the man confess his sins afore 't was
time t' mix the dope.

So Rustler Murphy answered, an' his voice
was clear an' strong
As he said: "Well, yes, I killed him, an' it
was a grievous wrong;
But I hope to be forgiven, for eternity is
long."

"Killed him! Who?" cried Buckskin Davis,
for he didn't understan'
(We were hangin' him for rustlin', not for
killin' of a man) ;
An' while killin' 's repperhensible, it 's
somethin' ye can stan'.

"What! Ain' you Rustler Murphy?" Davis
    asked him, wonder-eyed;
An' the feller looked confounded with sur-
    prise as he replied:
"No; my name is Texas Peters, an' I'm in
    for homicide."

For it seemed, back in the jail there, where
    the candle-light was dim,
We'd mistaken Texas Peters for the man
    t' fruit the limb,
An' in our agitation we had come nigh
    hangin' him!

So we humbly begged his pardon, an' we
    made him understan'
How we thought he was a horse-thief, when
    he only killed a man;
For, though killin' 's repperhensible, it 's
    somethin' ye can stan'.

—J. W. Foley

SORROWS OF WERTHER

Werther had a love for Charlotte
  Such as words could never utter;
Would you know how first he met her?
  She was cutting bread and butter.

Charlotte was a married lady,
  And a moral man was Werther,
And, for all the wealth of Indies,
  Would do nothing for to hurt her.

So he sighed and pined and ogled,
  And his passion boiled and bubbled,
Till he blew his silly brains out,
  And no more was by it troubled.

Charlotte, having seen his body
  Borne before her on a shutter.
Like a well-conducted person,
  Went on cutting bread and butter.

—William Makepeace Thackeray

FAITHLESS NELLY GRAY
A Pathetic Ballad

Ben Battle was a soldier bold,
　　And used to war's alarms:
But a cannon-ball took off his legs,
　　So he laid down his arms!

Now, as they bore him off the field,
　　Said he, "Let others shoot,
For here I leave my second leg,
　　And the Forty-second Foot!"

The army surgeons made him limbs:
　　Said he, "They're only pegs;
But there's as wooden members quite,
　　As represent my legs!"

Now Ben he loved a pretty maid,
　　Her name was Nelly Gray;
So he went to pay her his devours
　　When he'd devoured his pay!

But when he called on Nelly Gray,
　　She made him quite a scoff;
And when she saw his wooden legs,
　　Began to take them off!

"O Nelly Gray! O Nelly Gray!
    Is this your love so warm?
The love that loves a scarlet coat,
    Should be more uniform!"

Said she, "I loved a soldier once,
    For he was blithe and brave;
But I will never have a man
    With both legs in the grave!

Before you had those timber toes,
    Your love I did allow,
But then you know, you stand upon
    Another footing now!"

"O Nelly Gray! O Nelly Gray!
    For all your jeering speeches,
At duty's call I left my legs
    In Badajos's breaches!"

"Why, then," said she, "you've lost the feet
    Of legs in war's alarms,
And now you cannot wear your shoes
    Upon your feats of arms!"

"Oh, false and fickle Nelly Gray;
    I know why you refuse:

Though I've no feet—some other man
    Is standing in my shoes!

"I wish I ne'er had seen your face;
    But now a long farewell!
For you will be my death—alas!
    You will not be my Nell!

Now, when he went from Nelly Gray,
    His heart so heavy got—
And life was such a burden grown,
    It made him take a knot!

So round his melancholy neck
    A rope he did entwine,
And, for his second time in life
    Enlisted in the Line!

One end he tied around a beam,
    And then removed his pegs,
And as his legs were off,—of course,
    He soon was off his legs!

And there he hung till he was dead
    As any nail in town,—
For though distress had cut him up,
    It could not cut him down!

A dozen men sat on his corpse,
    To find out why he died—
And they buried Ben in four cross-roads,
    With a stake in his inside!

—Thomas Hood

THE OUTLANDISH KNIGHT

An outlandish knight came out of the North
    To woo a maiden fair,
He promised to take her to the North lands,
    Her father's only heir.

"Come, fetch me some of your father's gold,
    And some of your mother's fee;
And two of the best nags out of the stable,
    Where they stand thirty and three."

She fetched him some of her father's gold
    And some of her mother's fee;
And two of the best nags out of the stable,
    Where they stood thirty and three.

She mounted her on her milk-white steed,
    He on the dapple grey;

They rode till they came unto the sea-side,
    Three hours before it was day.

"Light off, light off thy milk-white steed,
    And deliver it unto me;
Six pretty maids have I drowned here,
    And thou the seventh shall be.

"Pull off, pull off thy silken gown,
    And deliver it unto me;
Methinks it looks too rich and too gay
    To rot in the salt sea.

"Pull off, pull off thy silken stays,
    And deliver them unto me;
Methinks they are too fine and gay
    To rot in the salt sea.

"Pull off, pull off thy Holland smock,
    And deliver it unto me;
Methinks it looks too rich and gay
    To rot in the salt sea."

"If I must pull off my Holland smock,
    Pray turn thy back unto me,
For it is not fitting that such a ruffian
    A woman unclad should see."

He turned his back towards her,
    And viewed the leaves so green;
She caught him round the middle so small,
    And tumbled him into the stream.

He dropped high, and he dropped low,
    Until he came to the tide—
"Catch hold of my hand, my pretty maiden,
    And I will make you my bride."

"Lie there, lie there, you false-hearted man,
    Lie there instead of me;
Six pretty maidens have you drowned here,
    And the seventh has drowned thee."

She mounted on her milk-white steed,
    And led the dapple grey.
She rode till she came to her father's hall,
    Three hours before it was day.

—Author Unknown

THE BRIEFLESS BARRISTER
A Ballad

An Attorney was taking a turn,
  In shabby habiliments drest;
His coat it was shockingly worn,
  And the rust had invested his vest.

His breeches had suffered a breach,
  His linen and worsted were worse;
He had scarce a whole crown in his hat,
  And not half-a-crown in his purse.

And thus as he wandered along,
  A cheerless and comfortless elf,
He sought for relief in a song,
  Or complainingly talked to himself:

"Unfortunate man that I am!
  I've never a client but grief;
The case is, I've no case at all,
  And in brief, I've ne'er had a brief!

"I've waited and waited in vain,
  Expecting an 'opening' to find,
Where an honest young lawyer might gain
  Some reward for the toil of his mind.

" 'Tis not that I'm wanting in law,
    Or lack an intelligent face,
That others have cases to plead,
    While I have to plead for a case.

"O, how can a modest young man
    E'er hope for the smallest progression—
The profession's already so full
    Of lawyers so full of profession!"

While thus he was strolling around,
    His eye accidentally fell
On a very deep hole in the ground,
    And he sighed to himself, "It is well!"

To curb his emotions, he sat
    On the curb-stone the space of a minute,
Then cried, "Here's an opening at last!"
    And in less than a jiffy was in it!

Next morning twelve citizens came
    ('Twas the coroner bade them attend),
To the end that it might be determined
    How the man had determined his end!

"The man was a lawyer, I hear,"
    Quoth the foreman who sat on the corse;
"A lawyer? Alas!" said another,
    "Undoubtedly he died of remorse!"

A third said, "He knew the deceased,
　　An attorney well versed in the laws,
And as to the cause of his death,
　　'Twas no doubt from the want of a cause."

The jury decided at length,
　　After solemnly weighing the matter,
"That the lawyer was drownded, because
　　He could not keep his head above water!"

—John G. Saxe

Gather up the Fragments

Mary Jane, the train is through yer:
Hallelujah, Hallelujah!
We will gather up the fragments that remain.
—A. E. HOUSMAN

THE REVOLVING DOOR

This is the horrible tale of Paul
MacGregor James D. Cuthbert Hall,
Who left his home one winter's day
To go to work, and on his way
In manner that was strange and weird
Mysteriously disappeared.
He left no clue, he left no trace,
He seemed to vanish into space.
Now listen to the fate of Paul
MacGregor James D. Cuthbert Hall.

He worked, did James, as shipping clerk
For Parkinson, McBaine & Burke,
Who in their store on North Broadway
Sold dry goods in a retail way.
And at the entrance to their store
There was a large revolving door
Through which passed all who went to work
For Parkinson, McBaine & Burke.

Upon this day, accursed of fate
MacGregor James, arriving late
Dashed headlong madly toward the store,
And plunged in through the spinning door
Around about it twirled and whirled
And Paul was twisted, curled and hurled,

And mashed, and crashed, and dashed, and bashed,
As round and round it spun and flashed.
At times it nearly stopped, and then
It straightway started up again.
"I fear that I'll be late for work,
And Parkinson, McBaine & Burke
Will be distressed and grieved," thought Paul
MacGregor James D. Cuthbert Hall.

He raised his voice in frantic cry,
And tried to hail the passers-by.
He tried in vain to call a cop,
But still the door refused to stop.
And so he spins and whirls about,
And struggles madly to get out,
While friends, heartbroken, search for Paul
MacGregor James D. Cuthbert Hall.

—Newman Levy

LITTLE WILLIE

Little Willie from his mirror
  Licked the mercury right off,
Thinking, in his childish error,
  It would cure the whooping cough.
At the funeral his mother
  Sadly said to Mrs. Brown:
" 'Twas a chilly day for Willie
When the mercury went down."

—Author Unknown

IN MEMORY OF ANNA HOPEWELL

Here lies the body of Anna
Done to death by a banana.
It wasn't the fruit that laid her low
But the skin of the thing that made her go.

—Author Unknown

CLOCK TIME BY THE GEYSER

There once was a man, named Power,
Went to see Old Faithful shower,
   But he slipped on a stone
   And fell in the cone——
Now you see him every hour on the hour.

—John White

GOLDEN GATES

Little Willie;
Pair of skates;
Hole in the ice;
Golden gates.

—Author Unknown

LITTLE WILLIE

Little Willie, mad as hell,
  Threw his sister down the well.
Mother said, when drawing water,
  "It's so hard to raise a daughter."

           —Author Unknown

A DOCTOR FELL IN A DEEP WELL

A doctor fell in a deep well,
  And broke his collarbone.
The Moral: Doctor, mind the sick
  And leave the well alone.

           —Author Unknown

BONES

Said Mr. Smith, "I really cannot
    Tell you, Dr. Jones—
The most peculiar pain I'm in—
    I think it's in my bones."

Said Dr. Jones, "Oh, Mr. Smith,
    That's nothing. Without doubt
We have a simple cure for that;
    It is to take them out."

He laid forthwith poor Mr. Smith
    Close-clamped upon the table,
And, cold as stone, took out his bone
    As fast as he was able.

And Smith said, "Thank you, thank you, thank you,"
    And wished him a Good-day;
And with his parcel 'neath his arm
    He slowly moved away.

—Walter de la Mare

SILLY WILLY

Willie's pa and ma were kind
So he never learned to mind.
Since he never took the whim
Willie never learned to swim.
Once, when Willie's yacht went down
Damned if Willie didn't drown.

—*R. L. B.*

EZRA SHANK

He rocked the boat
Did Ezra Shank.
These bubbles mark

      o

        o

       o

            Where Ezra sank.

—*Whiz Bang*

THERE WAS AN OLD LADY
NAMED CROCKETT

There was an Old Lady named Crockett
Who went to put a plug in a socket;
   But her hands were so wet
   She flew up like a jet
And came roaring back down like a rocket!

—William Jay Smith

AT GREAT TORRINGTON, DEVON

Here lies a man who was killed by lightning;
He died when his prospects seemed to be brightening.
He might have cut a flash in this world of trouble,
But the flash cut him, and he lies in the stubble.

—Author Unknown

THERE ONCE WAS A YOUNG MAN NAMED HALL

There once was a young man named Hall
Who fell in the spring in the fall.
   'Twould have been a sad thing
   Had he died in the spring
But he didn't—he died in the fall.

—Author Unknown

HE SHOT AT LEE WING

He shot at Lee Wing,
   But he winged Willie Wong;
A slight but regrettable
   Slip of the Tong.

—Author Unknown

THE SWIFT BULLETS

Gentle Jane once chanced to sit
Where some rifle bullets hit.
Though she had no bumps or sprains,
Gentle Jane felt shooting pains.

—Carolyn Wells

AT BOOT HILL IN TOMBSTONE, ARIZONA

Here lies Lester Moore
Four slugs from a .44
No Les
No More.

—Author Unknown

JOHN BUN

Here lies John Bun,
He was killed by a gun,
His name was not Bun, but Wood,
But Wood would not rhyme with gun,
    but Bun would.

—Author Unknown

EPITAPH

Insured for every accident
    And policies all paid for,
He drove as madly as he wished—
    Else what's insurance made for?

And then one day he hit a truck . . .
    Awhile his spirit hovered.
And now one reads above his head
    The words: "Completely covered."

—Richard Armour

RUTH AND JOHNNIE

Ruth and Johnnie,
  Side by side,
Went out for an
  Auto ride.
They hit a bump,
Ruth hit a tree,
And John kept going
  Ruthlessly.

—Author Unknown

SALLY SIMPKIN'S LAMENT

"Oh! what is that comes gliding in,
    And quite in middling haste?
It is the picture of my Jones,
    And painted to the waist.

"It is not painted to the life,
    For where's the trousers blue?
O Jones, my dear!—Oh, dear! my Jones,
    What is become of you?"

"O Sally, dear, it is too true,—
    The half that you remark
Is come to say my other half
    Is bit off by a shark!

"O Sally, sharks do things by halves,
    Yet most completely do!
A bite in one place seems enough,
    But I've been bit in two.

"You know I once was all your own,
    But now a shark must share!
But let that pass—for now to you
    I'm neither here nor there.

"Alas! death has a strange divorce
    Effected in the sea,

It has divided me from you,
  And even me from me!

"Don't fear my ghost will walk o' nights
  To haunt, as people say;
My ghost *can't* walk, for, oh! my legs
  Are many leagues away!

"Lord! think when I am swimming round,
  And looking where the boat is,
A shark just snaps away a *half,*
  Without *'a quarter's notice.'*

"One half is here, the other half
  Is near Columbia placed;
O Sally, I have got the whole
  Atlantic for my waist.

"But now, adieu—a long adieu!
  I've solved death's awful riddle,
And would say more, but I am doomed
  To break off in the middle!"

—*Thomas Hood*

HALLELUJAH!

"Hallelujah!" was the only observation
That escaped Lieutenant-Colonel Mary Jane,
When she tumbled off the platform in the station,
And was cut in little pieces by the train.
   Mary Jane, the train is through yer:
   Hallelujah, Hallelujah!
We will gather up the fragments that remain.

          —A. E. Housman

He Just Goes "Fffffff-ut!"

PRIMER OF CONSEQUENCES

Who plays with fire
Gets burned.
Who plays with knives
Gets cut.
And I have terrible, terrible qualms
About who plays with hydrogen bombs:
He just goes "fffffff-ut!"

—VIRGINIA BRASIER

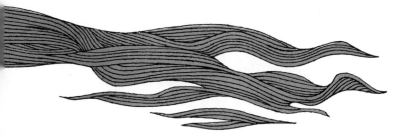

ATOMIC COURTESY

To smash the simple atom
All mankind was intent.
   Now any day
   The atom may
Return the compliment.

—*Ethel Jacobson*

ANY DAY NOW

Johnny reading in his comic
Learned to handle the atomic.
Johnny blew us all to vapors.
What a lad for cutting capers!

—*David McCord*

THE HYDROGEN DOG AND
THE COBALT CAT

The Hydrogen Dog and the Cobalt Cat
Side by side in the Armory sat.
Nobody thought about fusion or fission,
Everyone spoke of their peacetime mission,
    Till somebody came and opened the door.
There they were, in a neutron fog,
The Codrogen Cat and the Hybalt Dog;
    They mushroomed up with a terrible roar—
    And Nobody Never was there—Nomore.

—Frederick Winsor

RHYMES FOR A MODERN NURSERY

Little Miss Muffet
Crouched on a tuffet,
Collecting her shell-shocked wits.
There dropped (from a glider)
An H-bomb beside her—
Which frightened Miss Muffet to *bits*.

* * * *

In a cavern, in a canyon
Lay an unexploded mine,
Which was tripped on by Miss Shipton.
Dreadful sorry, Clementine.

—*Paul Dehn*

MOTHER GOOSE
(Circa 2054)

Humpty Dumpty sat on the wall,
A non-electro-magnetic ball.
All the Super's polariscopes
Couldn't revitalize his isotopes.

—*Irene Sekula*

SONG, ON READING THAT THE CYCLOTRON HAS PRODUCED COSMIC RAYS, BLASTED THE ATOM INTO TWENTY-TWO PARTICLES, SOLVED THE MYSTERY OF THE TRANSMUTATION OF ELEMENTS AND DEVIL KNOWS WHAT

Be gay, be merry, and don't be wary of milking the
    modest minute;
Rollick and frolic and carpe diem for all the fun that's
    in it;
Gather roses, or rose-red noses, and samba the night
    away:
There's nothing to fear but life and death—as far as
    we know today.

The lads in the lab are in high confab and the gods
    are huddled in holes;
There's a murmuration of trepidation among estab-
    lished souls;
The atom's groggy, the future foggy, so join your
    doggie at play:
There's nothing to fear but life and death—as far as
    we know today.

—Samuel Hoffenstein

IF THIS LITTLE WORLD TO-NIGHT

If this little world to-night
    Suddenly should fall thro' space
In a hissing, headlong flight,
    Shrivelling from off its face,
As it falls into the sun,
    In an instant every trace
Of the little crawling things—
    Ants, philosophers, and lice,
Cattle, cockroaches, and kings,
    Beggars, millionaires, and mice,
Men and maggots all as one
    As it falls into the sun—
Who can say but at the same
    Instant from some planet far
A child may watch us and exclaim:
    "See the pretty shooting star!"

—*Oliver Herford*

Mix You into Stuffin'

"You earnest Sage!" aloud they cried, "your book
you've read enough in!
We wish to chop you into bits and mix you
into Stuffin'!"

—EDWARD LEAR

THE STORY OF AUGUSTUS WHO WOULD
NOT HAVE ANY SOUP

Augustus was a chubby lad;
Fat ruddy cheeks Augustus had;
And everybody saw with joy,
The plump and hearty healthy boy.
He ate and drank as he was told,
And never let his soup get cold.
But one day, one cold winter's day,
He screamed out—"Take that soup away!
O take the nasty soup away!
I won't have any soup today!"

How lank and lean Augustus grows!
Next day he scarcely fills his clothes,
Yet, though he feels so weak and ill,
The naughty fellow cries out still—
"Not any soup for me, I say:
O take the nasty soup away!
I won't have any soup today!"

The third day comes; ah! what a sin!
To make himself so pale and thin.
Yet, when the soup is put on table,
He screams, as loud as he is able,
"Not any soup for me, I say:
O take the nasty soup away!
I won't have any soup today!"

71

Look at him, now the fourth day's come!
He scarcely weighs a sugar-plum;
He's like a little bit of thread,
And on the fifth day he was—dead!

—*Heinrich Hoffmann*

LITTLE BILLEE

There were three sailors of Bristol City
    Who took a boat and went to sea,
But first with beef and captain's biscuits,
    And pickled pork they loaded she.

There was gorging Jack, and guzzling Jimmy,
    And the youngest he was little Billee.
Now when they'd got as far as the Equator,
    They'd nothing left but one split pea.

Says gorging Jack to guzzling Jimmy,
    "I am extremely hungaree."
To gorging Jack says guzzling Jimmy,
    "We've nothing left, us must eat we."

Says gorging Jack to guzzling Jimmy,
    "With one another we shouldn't agree!

There's little Bill, he's young and tender,
   We're old and tough, so let's eat he."

"O Billy! we're going to kill and eat you,
   So undo the button of your chemie."
When Bill received this information,
   He used his pocket-handkerchie.

"First let me say my catechism,
   Which my poor mother taught to me."
"Make haste! make haste!" says guzzling Jimmy,
   While Jack pulled out his snicker-snee.

Then Bill went up to the main-top-gallant-mast,
   And down he fell on his bended knee,
He scarce had come to the Twelfth Commandment,
   When up he jumps—"There's land I see!"

"Jerusalem and Madagascar,
   And North and South Amerikee,
There's the British flag a-riding at anchor,
   With Admiral Napier, K.C.B."

So when they got aboard of the Admiral's,
   He hanged fat Jack and flogged Jimmee,
But as for little Bill, he made him
   The captain of a Seventy-three.

—*William Makepeace Thackeray*

FOLK SONG

At the boarding house where I live
Things are getting very old.
Long gray hairs are in the butter,
And the cheese is green with mold,
When the dog died we had sausage
When the cat died catnip tea.
When the landlord died I left it;
Spareribs are too much for me.

—Author Unknown

THERE WAS A YOUNG LADY OF RYDE

There was a Young Lady of Ryde
Who ate a green apple and died;
    The apple fermented
    Inside the lamented,
And made cider inside her inside.

—Author Unknown

VERDANCY

A green little boy in a green little way
A little green apple devoured one day;
And the little green grasses now tenderly wave
O'er the little green apple boy's green little grave.

—Author Unknown

THE LITTLE PEACH

A little peach in the orchard grew,—
A little peach of emerald hue;
Warmed by the sun and wet by the dew,
      It grew.

One day, passing that orchard through,
That little peach dawned on the view
Of Johnny Jones and his sister Sue—
      Them two.

Up at that peach a club they threw—
Down from the stem on which it grew
Fell that peach of emerald hue.
      Mon Dieu!

John took a bite and Sue a chew,
And then the trouble began to brew,—
Trouble the doctor couldn't subdue.
        Too true!

Under the turf where the daisies grew
They planted John and his sister Sue,
And their little souls to the angels flew,—
        Boo hoo!

What of that peach of the emerald hue,
Warmed by the sun, and wet by the dew?
Ah, well, its mission on earth is through.
        Adieu!

—*Eugene Field*

THE TWO OLD BACHELORS

Two old Bachelors were living in one house;
One caught a Muffin, the other caught a Mouse.
Said he who caught the Muffin to him who caught the
      Mouse,
"This happens just in time, for we've nothing in the
      house,
Save a tiny slice of lemon and a teaspoonful of honey,
And what to do for dinner—since we haven't any
      money?
And what can we expect if we haven't any dinner
But to lose our teeth and eyelashes and keep on growing
      thinner?"

Said he who caught the Mouse to him who caught the
      Muffin,
"We might cook this litte Mouse if we only had some
      stuffin'!
If we had but Sage and Onions we could do extremely
      well,
But how to get that Stuffin' it is difficult to tell!"

And then those two old Bachelors ran quickly to the
      town
And asked for Sage and Onions as they wandered up
      and down;

They borrowed two large Onions, but no Sage was to
  be found
In the Shops or in the Market or in all the Gardens
  round.

But someone said, "A hill there is, a little to the north,
And to its purpledicular top a narrow way leads forth;
And there among the rugged rocks abides an ancient
  Sage—
An earnest Man, who reads all day a most perplexing
  page.
Climb up and seize him by the toes—all studious as he
  sits—
And pull him down, and chop him into endless little
  bits!
Then mix him with your Onion (cut up likewise into
  scraps),
And your Stuffin' will be ready, and very good—
  perhaps."

And then those two old Bachelors, without loss of
  time,
The nearly purpledicular crags at once began to climb;
And at the top among the rocks, all seated in a nook,
They saw that Sage a-reading of a most enormous book.

"You earnest Sage!" aloud they cried, "your book
  you've read enough in!

We wish to chop you into bits and mix you into
Stuffin'!"
But that old Sage looked calmly up, and with his awful
book
At those two Bachelors' bald heads a certain aim he
took;
And over crag and precipice they rolled promiscuous
down—
At once they rolled, and never stopped in lane or field
or town;
And when they reached their house, they found (besides
their want of Stuffin')
The Mouse had fled—and previously had eaten up the
Muffin.

They left their home in silence by the once convivial
door;
And from that hour those Bachelors were never heard
of more.

—*Edward Lear*

PONJOO

My Uncle Jasper in Siam
Once breakfasted on Ponjoo jam.
This Ponjoo is a fruit, I find,
That has its pulp outside its rind,
   In colour a pale puce.
Within it lurks a heart-shaped stone
As hard as granite, iron, or bone,
   And round it wells its juice.

Now Uncle was a man of fashion
   Just visiting Siam;
And when he stripped away the pulp
And took the kernel at a gulp,
He flew into a furious passion
   And said the bad word '——!'

The Emperor, whose palace stood
Within the fragrant Ponjoo wood,
Sitting at lattice, stooped and heard
My uncle use this wicked word,
   And to his menials said:
'Convey that Pagan to a cell
Where never Echo's voice shall tell
The language that just now befell,
   And there strike off his head.'

And that is why our Family,
At early breakfast, lunch, or tea,
    And I, where'er I am,
If on the table we see laid
A pot of Ponjoo marmalade,
Say, 'Drat it,' to the parlour-maid,
    But never, never '———!'

—*Walter de la Mare*

COMMISSARY REPORT

Our fathers were fellows of substance and weight,
They drank when they drank, and they ate when they
                    ate,
They made a light breakfast of flapjacks and pie,
They greeted corned beef with a ravenous cry,
Their luncheon was spareribs, with beans on the side—
    They lived free and equal,
    And what was the sequel?
They died.

The men of our era are timid with food,
Their principal ration is calories, stewed,
They start off the morning with prune flakes and bran

And patented mannas,
And shredded bananas—
They get a whole meal from a single tin can.
They keep a keen eye on the vitamin chart,
Affect fancy diets, and know them by heart,
They pick at their food like a wren or a chick
For fear they'll get cancer
And what is the answer?
They're sick.

—*Stoddard King*

A CERTAIN YOUNG MAN OF GREAT GUMPTION

A certain young man of great gumption,
Among cannibals had the presumption
To go—but, alack!
He never came back.
They say 'twas a case of consumption.

—*Author Unknown*

from SOME LITTLE BUG

In these days of indigestion
It is oftentimes a question
   As to what to eat and what to leave alone;
For each microbe and bacillus
Has a different way to kill us,
   And in time they always claim us for their own.
There are germs of every kind
In any food that you can find
   In the market or upon the bill of fare.
Drinking water's just as risky
As the so-called deadly whiskey,
   And it's often a mistake to breathe the air.

Some little bug is going to find you some day,
Some little bug will creep behind you some day,
   Then he'll send for his bug friends
   And all your earthly trouble ends;
Some little bug is going to find you some day.

—Roy Atwell

A PARADOX

Though we boast of modern progress as aloft we
proudly soar;
Above untutored cannibals whose habits we deplore,
Yet in our daily papers any day you chance to look
You may find this advertisement: "Wanted—A girl to
cook."

—*Judge* (1894)

A POE—'EM OF PASSION

It was many and many a year ago,
    On an island near the sea,
That a maiden lived whom you mightn't know
    By the name of Cannibalee;
And this maiden she lived with no other thought
    Than a passionate fondness for me.

I was a child, and she was a child—
    Tho' her tastes were adult Feejee—
But she loved with a love that was more than love,
    My yearning Cannibalee;
With a love that could take me roast or fried
    Or raw, as the case might be.

And that is the reason that long ago,
   In that island near the sea,
I had to turn the tables and eat
   My ardent Cannibalee—
Not really because I was fond of her,
   But to check her fondness for me.

But the stars never rise but I think of the size
   Of my hot-potted Cannibalee;
And the moon never stares but it brings me nightmares
   Of my spare-rib Cannibalee;
And all the night-tide she is restless inside,
Is my still indigestible dinner-belle bride,
In her pallid tomb, which is *Me*—
In her solemn sepulcher, *Me*.

             —*C. F. Lummis*

Shiverous Beasts

. . . not even the last clap of doom
  Could be heard through his blabberous laugh.
Nothing human could live through its boom.
  —JOHN CIARDI

HOW DOTH THE LITTLE CROCODILE

How doth the little crocodile
Improve his shining tail,
And pour the waters of the Nile
On every golden scale!

How cheerfully he seems to grin,
How neatly spreads his claws,
And welcomes little fishes in
With gently smiling jaws!

—*Lewis Carroll*

THE MONKEYS AND THE CROCODILE

Five little monkeys
Swinging from a tree;
Teasing Uncle Crocodile,
Merry as can be.
Swinging high, swinging low,
Swinging left and right:
"Dear Uncle Crocodile,
Come and take a bite!"

Five little monkeys
Swinging in the air;

Heads up, tails up,
    Little do they care.
Swinging up, swinging down,
    Swinging far and near:
"Poor Uncle Crocodile,
    Aren't you hungry, dear?"

Four little monkeys
    Sitting in the tree;
Heads down, tails down,
    Dreary as can be.
Weeping loud, weeping low,
    Crying to each other:
"Wicked Uncle Crocodile,
    To gobble up our brother!"

—*Laura E. Richards*

ALGY

Algy saw a bear;
The bear saw Algy.
The bear had a bulge;
The bulge was Algy.

—*Folk Rhyme*

B STANDS FOR BEAR

When Bears are seen
    Approaching in the distance,
Make up your mind at once between
    Retreat and Armed Resistance.

A Gentleman remained to fight—
    With what result for him?
The Bear, with ill-conceived delight,
    Devoured him, Limb by Limb.

Another Person turned and ran;
    He ran extremely hard:
The Bear was faster than the Man,
    And beat him by a yard.

MORAL

Decisive action in the hour of need
Denotes the Hero, but does not succeed.

—Hilaire Belloc

LITTLE KATY

Little Katy wandered where
She espied a grizzly bear;
Noticing his savage wrath,
Katy kicked him from her path.

Little Katy, darling child,
Met a leopard, fierce and wild;
Ere the ugly creature sped off,
Little Katy bit his head off.

—Author Unknown

THE LION

The Lion is a kingly beast.
He likes a Hindu for a feast.
And if no Hindu he can get,
The lion-family is upset.

He cuffs his wife and bites her ears
Till she is nearly moved to tears.
Then some explorer finds the den
And all is family peace again.

—Vachel Lindsay

from ADVENTURES OF ISABEL

Isabel met an enormous bear,
Isabel, Isabel, didn't care;
The bear was hungry, the bear was ravenous,
The bear's big mouth was cruel and cavernous.
The bear said, "Isabel, glad to meet you,
How do, Isabel, now I'll eat you!"
Isabel, Isabel, didn't worry,
Isabel didn't scream or scurry.
She washed her hands and she straightened her hair up,
Then Isabel quietly ate the bear up.

—Ogden Nash

THE LION

Oh, weep for Mr. and Mrs. Bryan!
He was eaten by a lion;
Following which, the lion's lioness
Up and swallowed Bryan's Bryaness.

—Ogden Nash

THERE WAS A YOUNG LADY OF NIGER

There was a young lady of Niger
Who smiled as she rode on a Tiger;
   They came back from the ride
   With the lady inside,
And the smile on the face of the Tiger.

—Author Unknown

A BOSTON BOY WENT OUT TO YUMA

A Boston boy went out to Yuma
And there he encountered a puma—
   And later they found
   Just a spot on the ground,
And a puma in very good huma.

—D. D. in Boston Transcript

THE FLATTERED FLYING FISH

Said the Shark to the Flying Fish over the Phone:
"Will you join me tonight? I am dining alone.
Let me order a nice little dinner for two!
And come as you are, in your shimmering blue."

Said the Flying Fish: "Fancy remembering me,
And the dress I wore at the Porpoises' tea!"
"How could I forget?" said the Shark in his guile:
"I expect you at eight!" and rang off with a smile.

She has powdered her nose; she has put on her things;
She is off with one flap of her luminous wings.
O little one, lovely, light-hearted and vain,
The Moon will not shine on your beauty again!

—*E. V. Rieu*

THE RHYME OF THE CHIVALROUS SHARK

Most chivalrous fish of the ocean,
   To ladies forbearing and mild,
Though his record be dark, is the man-eating shark
   Who will eat neither woman nor child.

He dines upon seamen and skippers,
   And tourists his hunger assuage,
And a fresh cabin boy will inspire him with joy
   If he's past the maturity age.

A doctor, a lawyer, a preacher,
   He'll gobble one any fine day,
But the ladies, God bless 'em, he'll only address 'em
   Politely and go on his way.

I can readily cite you an instance
   Where a lovely young lady of Breem,
Who was tender and sweet and delicious to eat,
   Fell into the bay with a scream.

She struggled and flounced in the water
   And signaled in vain for her bark,
And she'd surely been drowned if she hadn't been found
   By a chivalrous man-eating shark.

He bowed in a manner most polished,
   Thus soothing her impulses wild;

"Don't be frightened," he said, "I've been properly bred
And will eat neither woman nor child."

Then he proffered his fin and she took it—
Such a gallantry none can dispute—
While the passengers cheered as the vessel they neared
And a broadside was fired in salute.

And they soon stood alongside the vessel,
When a life-saving dingey was lowered
With the pick of the crew, and her relatives, too,
And the mate and the skipper aboard.

So they took her aboard in a jiffy,
And the shark stood attention the while,
Then he raised on his flipper and ate up the skipper
And went on his way with a smile.

And this shows that the prince of the ocean,
To ladies forbearing and mild,
Though his record be dark, is the man-eating shark
Who will eat neither woman nor child.

—*Wallace Irwin*

from THE UNTUTORED GIRAFFE

Once on a time a young Giraffe
(Who when at school devoured the chaff
And trampled underneath his feet
The golden grains of Learning's wheat)
Upon his travels chanced to see
A Python hanging from a tree,
A thing he'd never met before,
All neck it seemed and nothing more;
And stranger still it was bestrown
With pretty spots, much like his own.
"Well, well! I've often heard," he said,
"Of foolish folk who lose their head;
But really it's a funnier joke
To meet a head that's lost its folk!"

—Oliver Herford

AWAY WITH BLOODSHED

Away with bloodshed, I love not such,
But Jane Eliza snores too much.

I bought a serpent that bites and stings
For three-and-sixpence or four shillings.

When Jane Eliza began to snore
I put it under her bedroom door.

The serpent had neither bit nor stung,
It had only just put out its tongue,

When Jane Eliza fell out of bed
And bumped upon it and killed it dead.

It showed off none of its pretty tricks
That cost four shillings or three-and-six;

It had no time to sting or bite
Nor even to utter the words "Good night."

So three-and-sixpence at least is gone,
And Jane Eliza, she still snores on.

—*A. E. Housman*

LITTLE BOYS OF TEXAS

The little boys of Texas prance
To swimming places without their pants
And dive in deep to cool their souls
In very dubious swimming-holes.

The checkered rattlesnake hides there,
He does not ever care to share
His water, slimy as can be,
With any Christian company.

The diamond-back whose single bite
Is full of everlasting night
Lurks beside the sunken log,
Short-tempered as the love-crossed dog.

The hoop-snake puts her sharp tail in
Her mouth and rolls as fast as sin
To be at the water bright and smart
With murder at her slender heart.

And there the deadly cotton-mouth,
Honey-mannered as the South,
Lies saying, "You-all sure are sweet!"
And stabs quick death into your feet.

But boys of Texas do not fret
So long's the water there is wet,
They drink in quarts of typhoid fever,
And laugh and yell without a quiver.

They never mind a bitten toe,
These grandsons of the Alamo,
They are tough as spikes and nails,
These Davy Crocketts with hard tails.

And when they leave the slimy bank,
There they lie, stiff, rank on rank—
Cotton-mouth, rattler, hoop, outspread,
Sadder, wiser, and plumb dead!

—Robert P. Tristram Coffin

THE TERMITE

Some primal termite knocked on wood
And tasted it, and found it good,
And that is why your Cousin May
Fell through the parlor floor to-day.

—Ogden Nash

LANCASTER COUNTY TRAGEDY

Pennsylvania Dutch Mouse
Is mourned by all his kin.
He should have gone the door out
But he went the house cat in.

—*W. Lowrie Kay*

THE KILKENNY CATS

There wanst was two cats at Kilkenny,
Each thought there was one cat too many,
So they quarrell'd and fit,
They scratch'd and they bit,
Till, excepting their nails,
And the tips of their tails,
Instead of two cats, there warnt any.

—*Author Unknown*

AN ELEGY ON THE DEATH OF A MAD DOG

Good people all, of every sort,
   Give ear unto my song;
And if you find it wondrous short
   It cannot hold you long.

In Islington there was a man
   Of whom the world might say
That still a godly race he ran
   Whene'er he went to pray.

A kind and gentle heart he had,
   To comfort friends and foes;
The naked every day he clad,
   When he put on his clothes.

And in that town a dog was found,
   As many dogs there be,
Both mongrel, puppy, whelp, and hound,
   And curs of low degree.

This dog and man at first were friends,
   But when a pique began,
The dog, to gain his private ends,
   Went mad, and bit the man.

Around from all the neighbouring streets
    The wondering neighbours ran,
And swore the dog had lost his wits
    To bite so good a man.

The wound it seemed both sore and sad
    To every Christian eye;
And while they swore the dog was mad,
    They swore the man would die.

But soon a wonder came to light,
    That show'd the rogues they lied:
The man recover'd of the bite,
    The dog it was that died.

—*Oliver Goldsmith*

ON FELL

While Fell was reposing himself on the hay,
A reptile conceal'd bit his leg as he lay;
But all venom himself of the wound he made light,
And got well, while the scorpion died of the bite.

—*From the German of Lessing*

ON A MONUMENT IN FRANCE WHICH MARKS THE LAST RESTING PLACE OF AN ARMY MULE

In memory of Maggie
   Who In Her Time Kicked
Two Colonels, Four Majors, 10 Captains,
24 Lieutenants, 42 Sergeants,
    432 Other Ranks
  And One Mills Bomb

—Author Unknown

THE OLD LADY WHO SWALLOWED A FLY

I know an old lady who swallowed a fly,
I don't know why she swallowed the fly.
I guess she'll die.

I know an old lady who swallowed a spider;
It wrickles and ickles and tickles inside 'er.
She swallowed the spider to catch the fly;
I don't know why she swallowed the fly.
I guess she'll die.

I know an old lady who swallowed a bird;
She swallowed a bird, my! how absurd.

She swallowed the bird to catch the spider;
It wrickles and ickles and tickles inside 'er.
She swallowed the spider to catch the fly;
I don't know why she swallowed the fly.
I guess she'll die.

I know an old lady who swallowed a cat;
She swallowed a cat, imagine that!
She swallowed the cat to catch the bird.
She swallowed a bird, my! how absurd.
She swallowed the bird to catch the spider;
It wrickles and ickles and tickles inside 'er.
She swallowed the spider to catch the fly;
I don't know why she swallowed the fly;
I guess she'll die.

I know an old lady who swallowed a dog;
She swallowed a dog—my, what a hog!
She swallowed the dog to catch the cat;
She swallowed a cat, imagine that!
She swallowed the cat to catch the bird;
She swallowed a bird, my! how absurd.
She swallowed the bird to catch the spider;
It wrickles and ickles and tickles inside 'er.
She swallowed the spider to catch the fly;
I don't know why she swallowed the fly.
I guess she'll die.

I know an old lady who swallowed a goat;
She swallowed a goat—it got stuck in her throat.
She swallowed the goat to catch the dog;
She swallowed a dog—my, what a hog!
She swallowed the dog to catch the cat;
She swallowed a cat, imagine that!
She swallowed the cat to catch the bird;
She swallowed a bird, my! how absurd.
She swallowed the bird to catch the spider;
It wrickles and ickles and tickles inside 'er.
She swallowed the spider to catch the fly;
I don't know why she swallowed the fly.
I guess she'll die.

I know an old lady who swallowed a horse.
She died, of course.

—*Author Unknown*

Such a Pleasant Familee

"...her unpleasant habits seem
    Quite curious to me—
Considering she came from such
    A pleasant familee."
                    —WALLACE IRWIN

SIMILIA SIMILIBUS

There was a jolly student with a medical degree,
Who talked of naught the livelong day save man's
anatomy,
Until at last his grandpa,
A learnèd man forsooth,
Concluded he would end things
And sit down upon the youth.

Said he, "I ne'er will argue with a verdant youth like
him,
But I'll hem him round with learnèd saws and proverbs
old and grim.
Each argument he offers
I'll crush with adage quaint
Till he's not a leg to stand on
And has learned some self-restraint."

The maxims swarmed like hornets, the axioms like bees,
With a thought from Aristotle and a line from Socrates,
He dazed him with an adage
Till he'd time to pick a flaw;
Then he ended up the battle,
And he did it with a saw.

But that night a muffled figure stole into the old man's
room,

And on that ancient gentleman did work amidst the
    gloom
With great medical precision
        And with glee that fiends would awe
Till he'd not a leg to stand on,
        And—he did it with a saw.

—John Hunt Morgan

LIZZIE BORDEN

Lizzie Borden took an axe
And gave her mother forty whacks;
When she saw what she had done
She gave her father forty-one!

—Author Unknown

LITTLE WILLIE

Little Willie, once in ire
Threw his sister in the fire.
His mother said, above her screams,
"He's really nicer than he seems."

—Author Unknown

JIM, WHO RAN AWAY FROM HIS NURSE, AND WAS EATEN BY A LION

There was a Boy whose name was Jim;
His Friends were very good to him.
They gave him Tea, and Cakes, and Jam,
And slices of delicious Ham,
And Chocolate with pink inside,
And little Tricycles to ride,
And
   read him Stories through and through,
And even took him to the Zoo—
But there it was the dreadful Fate
Befell him, which I now relate.

You know—at least you *ought* to know,
For I have often told you so—

That Children never are allowed
To leave their Nurses in a Crowd;
Now this was Jim's especial Foible,
He ran away when he was able,
And on this inauspicious day
He slipped his hand and ran away!
He hadn't gone a yard when—
                            Bang!
With open Jaws, a Lion sprang,
And hungrily began to eat
The Boy: beginning at his feet.

Now just imagine how it feels
When first your toes and then your heels,
And then by gradual degrees,
Your shins and ankles, calves and knees,
Are slowly eaten, bit by bit.

No wonder Jim detested it!
No wonder that he shouted "Hi!"
The Honest Keeper heard his cry,
Though very fat
                    he almost ran
To help the little gentleman.
"Ponto!" he ordered as he came
(For Ponto was the Lion's name),
"Ponto!" he cried,
                        with angry frown.

"Let go, Sir! Down, Sir! Put it down!"

The Lion made a sudden Stop,
He let the Dainty Morsel drop,
And slunk reluctant to his Cage,
Snarling with Disappointed Rage
But when he bent him over Jim
The Honest Keeper's
                eyes were dim.
The Lion having reached his Head,
The Miserable Boy was dead!

When Nurse informed his Parents, they
Were more Concerned than I can say:—
His Mother, as She dried her eyes,
Said, "Well—it gives me no surprise,
He would not do as he was told!"
His Father, who was self-controlled,
Bade all the children round attend
To James' miserable end,
And always keep a-hold of Nurse
For fear of finding something worse.

—*Hilaire Belloc*

JOHNNY

Johnny used to find content
In standing always rather bent,
Like an inverted letter *J*.
His angry relatives would say,
"Stand up! don't slouch! You've got a spine,
Stand like a lamppost, not a vine!"
One day they heard an awful crack—
He'd stood up straight—it broke his back!

—Emma Rounds

DUST

Agatha Morley
All her life
Grumbled at dust
Like a good wife.

Dust on a table,
Dust on a chair,
Dust on a mantel
She couldn't bear.

She forgave faults
In man and child
But a dusty shelf
Would set her wild.

She bore with sin
Without protest,
But dust thoughts preyed
Upon her rest.

Agatha Morley
Is sleeping sound
Six feet under
The mouldy ground.

Six feet under
The earth she lies
With dust at her feet
And dust in her eyes.

—Sydney King Russell

HENRY KING, WHO CHEWED BITS OF STRING, AND WAS EARLY CUT OFF IN DREADFUL AGONIES

The Chief Defect of Henry King
Was chewing little bits of String.
At last he swallowed some which tied
Itself in ugly Knots inside.
Physicians of the Utmost Fame
Were called at once; but when they came
They answered, as they took their Fees,
"There is no Cure for this Disease.
Henry will very soon be dead."
His Parents stood about his Bed
Lamenting his Untimely Death,
When Henry, with his Latest Breath,
Cried—"Oh, my Friends, be warned by me,
That Breakfast, Dinner, Lunch and Tea
Are all the Human Frame requires . . ."
With that the Wretched Child expires.

—Hilaire Belloc

YOU'D SAY IT WAS A FUNERAL

You'd say it was a funeral, a funeral,
　　So dreary and so dim,
　　So ghoulish and so grim
Is the conversation, the conversation
　　Of Mr. and Mrs. Mimm.

Of accidents, bad accidents,
　　Of widows, wars and wills,
Of tragedy, dark tragedy,
　　And chills and pills and bills,
　　Of doctoring and lawyering
　　And quarrelling so dire,
Of burying, sad burying,
　　And farms on fire.
Of sickness and starvation
　　And all things grave and grim,
Of such is the conversation
　　Of Mr. and Mrs. Mimm.

—James Reeves

THE BATH

Broad is the Gate and wide the Path
That leads man to his daily bath;
But ere you spend the shining hour
With plunge and spray, with sluice and show'r—

With all that teaches you to dread
The bath as little as your bed—
Remember, whereso'er you be,
To shut the door and turn the key!

I had a friend—my friend no more!—
Who failed to bolt the bath-room door;

A maiden-aunt of his, one day,
Walked in, as half-submerged he lay!

But did not notice nephew John,
And turned the boiling water on!

He had no time, or even scope,
To camouflage himself with soap,
But gave a yell and flung aside
The sponge, 'neath which he sought to hide!

It fell to earth, I know not where!
He beat his breast in his despair,
And then, like Venus from the foam,
Sprang into view, and made for home!

His aunt fell fainting to the ground!
Alas! They never brought her round!

She died, intestate, in her prime,
The victim of another's crime;

And John can never quite forget
How, by a breach of etiquette,
He lost, at one fell swoop (or plunge)
His aunt, his honour, and his sponge!

—*Harry Graham*

THE EEL

There was an old person of Dover
Who called on his sister in Deal,
With a sack hanging over his shoulder
In which was a whopping great eel.
It leapt down the area, scuttled upstairs,
It golloped up bolsters and wash-jugs and chairs,
Her boots, shoes, and slippers, in singles and pairs;
And alas! when this Ogre
Had finished its meal,
There was no-one of Dover
With a sister in Deal.

—Walter de la Mare

BROTHER AND SISTER

"Sister, sister, go to bed!
Go and rest your weary head."
Thus the prudent brother said.

"Do you want a battered hide,
Or scratches to your face applied?"
Thus his sister calm replied.

"Sister, do not raise my wrath.
I'd make you into mutton broth
As easily as kill a moth!"

The sister raised her beaming eye
And looked on him indignantly
And sternly answered, "Only try!"

Off to the cook he quickly ran.
"Dear Cook, pray lend a frying-pan
To me as quickly as you can."

"And wherefore should I lend it you?"
"The reason, Cook, is plain to view.
I wish to make an Irish stew."

"What meat is in that stew to go?"
"My sister'll be the contents!"
                              "Oh!"
"You'll lend the pan to me, Cook?"
                              "No!"

Moral: Never stew your sister.

—*Lewis Carroll*

THE TWINS

In form and feature, face and limb,
  I grew so like my brother,
That folks got taking me for him,
  And each for one another.
It puzzled all our kith and kin,
  It reached an awful pitch;
For one of us was born a twin,
  Yet not a soul knew which.

One day (to make the matter worse),
  Before our names were fixed,
As we were being washed by nurse
  We got completely mixed;
And thus, you see, by Fate's decree,
  (Or rather nurse's whim),
My brother John got christened *me*,
  And I got christened *him*.

This fatal likeness even dogg'd
  My footsteps when at school,
And I was always getting flogg'd,
  For John turned out a fool.
I put this question hopelessly
  To everyone I knew—
What *would* you do, if you were me,
  To prove that you were *you*?

Our close resemblance turned the tide
    Of my domestic life;
For somehow my intended bride
    Became my brother's wife.
In short, year after year the same
    Absurd mistake went on;
And when I died—the neighbors came
    And buried brother John!

—*Henry S. Leigh*

THE PURIST

I give you now Professor Twist,
A conscientious scientist.
Trustees exclaimed, "He never bungles."
And sent him off to distant jungles.
Camped on a tropic riverside,
One day he missed his loving bride.
She had, the guide informed him later,
Been eaten by an alligator.
Professor Twist could not but smile.
"You mean," he said, "a crocodile."

—*Ogden Nash*

125

WILLS

Men, dying, make their wills—but wives
    Escape a work so sad;
Why should they make what all their lives
    The gentle dames have had.

—John G. Saxe

ON THE WIFE OF A PARISH CLERK

The children of Israel wanted bread,
    And the Lord he sent them manna,
Old clerk Wallace wanted a wife,
    And the Devil he sent him Anna.

—Author Unknown

A REASONABLE AFFLICTION

On his death-bed poor Lubin lies;
    His spouse is in despair:
With frequent sobs, and mutual cries,
    They both express their care.

"A different cause," says Parson Sly,
    "The same effect may give:
Poor Lubin fears that he shall die;
    His wife, that he may live."

—*Matthew Prior*

AUNT ELIZA

Willie pushed his Aunt Eliza
Off a rock into a geyser,
Now he's feeling quite dejected,
Didn't get the rise that he expected.

—*Author Unknown*

AUNT MAUD

I had written to Aunt Maud
Who was on a trip abroad,
When I heard she'd died of cramp
Just too late to save the stamp.

—Author Unknown

THE CARELESS NIECE

Once her brother's child, for fun,
Pointed at her aunt a gun.
At this conduct of her niece's
Gentle Jane went all to pieces.

—Carolyn Wells

THE PYTHON

A Python I should not advise,—
It needs a doctor for its eyes,
And has the measles yearly.
However if you feel inclined
To get one (to improve your mind,
And not from fashion merely),
Allow no music near its cage;
And when it flies into a rage
Chastise it, most severely.

I had an aunt in Yucatan
Who bought a Python from a man
    And kept it for a pet.
She died, because she never knew
These simple little rules and few;—
    The Snake is living yet.

—*Hilaire Belloc*

from SCIENCE FOR THE YOUNG

Arthur with a lighted taper
Touched the fire to grandpa's paper.
Grandpa leaped a foot or higher,
Dropped the sheet and shouted "Fire!"
Arthur, wrapped in contemplation,
Viewed the scene of conflagration.
"This," he said "confirms my notion—
Heat creates both light and motion."

—Wallace Irwin

POOR GRANDPA

Grandpa died on his vacation,
　　Everyone felt sad,
'Cause it was the last vacation
　　Grandpa ever had.

—R. C. O'Brien

SUCH A PLEASANT FAMILEE

"Her Pa committed suicide
    By biting off his head.
Her mother saw her uncle's ghost
    And died of fright," he said,
"So her unpleasant habits seem
    Quite curious to me—
Considering she came from such
    A pleasant familee."

—Wallace Irwin

Go *Doucement, Doucement* to the Cemetery

. . . When a rich man dies, they
drag out the Sacrament
and a golden Cross, and go doucement, doucement
to the cemetery.

—ROBERT CREELEY

FOR A PESSIMIST

He wore his coffin for a hat,
    Calamity his cape,
While on his face a death's head sat
And waved a bit of crape.

—Countee Cullen

ON SEEING A POMPOUS FUNERAL
FOR A BAD HUSBAND

"Why for your spouse this pompous fuss?
Was he not all your life a curse?
Did he not tease, and scold, and fight,
And plague you, morning, noon and night?"
"True, but at length one single action
Made up for each past malefaction."
"Indeed, what was this action, pray?"
"Why sir, it was—he died one day!"

—Author Unknown

135

DONNE REDONE

Ask not for whom the bells toll.
Don't get yourself in a stew.
As long as you can hear the clang,
Relax; they're not for you.

—Joseph Paul Tierney

WAKE

Tell all my mourners
To mourn in red—
Cause there ain't no sense
In my bein' dead.

—Langston Hughes

IT ISN'T THE COUGH

It isn't the cough
That carries you off;
It's the coffin
They carry you off in.

—Author Unknown

MADRIGAL MACABRE

Some want a vault, some want a grave,
Bold sailors the sepulchral wave;
To some cold lives it has hotly mattered
That they be burned and their ashes scattered;
Some souls bemused with fear of haunts
Want to be buried beside their aunts;
Most urban jokers, treys and deuces
Want to be laid under hometown spruces;
Pharaohs stanch and Pharaohs fickle
Agreed upon a permanent pickle,
Surrounded by such lesser dills
As needful to their royal wills;
Some want a headstone, some a slab,
Some flowers, some rice—as good, but drab;
Some want a funeral de luxe,
Some specify but dogs and cooks;
Some want violent lamentation,
Some a muted murmuration;
Some wills grow jolly and complete
With wakes and hot, baked funeral meat,
With women keening and men drinking
And the corpse, as it imagines, winking;
Some want show and some deceases
Want neither choir nor Rest-in-Peaces;
Some, dying, feel their own tears flow
At thought of a pal saying, "Good old Joe!"

Some will not close a final eye
Until assured their graves are dry;
Some who know gardens and manure
Are partial to damp sepulture;
Some would like the works entire,
Burial, mausoleum, pyre,
The gloved cortege, the plumèd horse,
The lodges out in splendid force—
But I, who have but thinly thrived,
Should much prefer to be revived.

—Samuel Hoffenstein

JERRY JONES

Six feet beneath
This funeral wreath
Is laid upon the shelf
One Jerry Jones,
Who dealt in bones,
And now he's bones himself.

—Author Unknown

HELL'S BELLS

The ambulance flies at a furious gait
That registers utter defiance of Fate
As clanging through traffic quite agile and supple,
It picks up one person and knocks down a couple.

—Margaret Fishback

THE JILTED FUNERAL

Why does this seedy lady look
As though she should be undertook?
Ah, should her spirit now forsake her,
I wouldn't want to undertake her!

—Gelett Burgess

THE CREMATION OF SAM McGEE

There are strange things done in the midnight sun
  By the men who moil for gold;
The Arctic trails have their secret tales
  That would make your blood run cold;
The Northern Lights have seen queer sights,
  But the queerest they ever did see
Was that night on the marge of Lake Lebarge
  I cremated Sam McGee.

Now Sam McGee was from Tennessee, where
      the cotton blooms and blows.
Why he left his home in the South to roam
      'round the Pole, God only knows.
He was always cold, but the land of gold seemed
      to hold him like a spell;
Though he'd often say in his homely way that
      "he'd sooner live in hell."

On a Christmas Day we were mushing our way
      over the Dawson trail.
Talk of your cold! through the parka's fold it
      stabbed like a driven nail.
If our eyes we'd close, then the lashes froze till
      sometimes we couldn't see;
It wasn't much fun, but the only one to whimper
      was Sam McGee.

And that very night, as we lay packed tight in
    our robes beneath the snow,
And the dogs were fed, and the stars o'erhead
    were dancing heel and toe,
He turned to me, and "Cap," says he, "I'll cash
    in this trip, I guess;
And if I do, I'm asking that you won't refuse my
    last request."

Well, he seemed so low that I couldn't say no;
    then he says with a sort of moan:
"It's the cursèd cold, and it's got right hold till
    I'm chilled clean through to the bone.
Yet 'tain't being dead—it's my awful dread of
    the icy grave that pains;
So I want you to swear that, foul or fair, you'll
    cremate my last remains."

A pal's last need is a thing to heed, so I swore
    I would not fail;
And we started on at the streak of dawn; but
    God! he looked ghastly pale.
He crouched on the sleigh, and he raved all day
    of his home in Tennessee;
And before nightfall a corpse was all that was
    left of Sam McGee.

There wasn't a breath in that land of death, and
    I hurried, horror-driven,

With a corpse half hid that I couldn't get rid,
    because of a promise given;
It was lashed to the sleigh, and it seemed to say:
    "You may tax your brawn and brains,
But you promised true, and it's up to you to
    cremate those last remains."

Now a promise made is a debt unpaid, and the
    trail has its own stern code.
In the days to come, though my lips were dumb,
    in my heart how I cursed that load.
In the long, long night, by the lone firelight,
    while the huskies, round in a ring,
Howled out their woes to the homeless snows
    —O God! how I loathed the thing.

And every day that quiet clay seemed to heavy
    and heavier grow;
And on I went, though the dogs were spent and
    the grub was getting low;
The trail was bad, and I felt half mad, but I
    swore I would not give in;
And I'd often sing to the hateful thing, and it
    hearkened with a grin.

Till I came to the marge of Lake Lebarge, and
    a derelict there lay;
It was jammed in the ice, but I saw in a trice it
    was called the *Alice May*.

And I looked at it, and I thought a bit, and I
  looked at my frozen chum;
Then "Here," said I, with a sudden cry, "is
  my cre-ma-tor-eum."

Some planks I tore from the cabin floor, and I
  lit the boiler fire;
Some coal I found that was lying around, and I
  heaped the fuel higher;
The flames just soared, and the furnace roared
  —such a blaze you seldom see;
And I burrowed a hole in the glowing coal, and
  I stuffed in Sam McGee.

Then I made a hike, for I didn't like to hear him
  sizzle so;
And the heavens scowled, and the huskies
  howled, and the wind began to blow.
It was icy cold, but the hot sweat rolled down my
  cheeks, and I don't know why;
And the greasy smoke in an inky cloak went
  streaking down the sky.

I do not know how long in the snow I wrestled
  with grisly fear;
But the stars came out and they danced about
  ere again I ventured near;
I was sick with dread, but I bravely said: "I'll
  just take a peep inside.

I guess he's cooked, and it's time I looked";...
    then the door I opened wide.

And there sat Sam, looking cool and calm, in the
        heart of the furnace roar;
And he wore a smile you could see a mile, and
        he said: "Please close that door.
It's fine in here, but I greatly fear you'll let in
        the cold and storm—
Since I left Plumtree, down in Tennessee, it's
        the first time I've been warm."

There are strange things done in the midnight sun
    By the men who moil for gold;
The Arctic trails have their secret tales
    That would make your blood run cold;
The Northern Lights have seen queer sights,
    But the queerest they ever did see
Was that night on the marge of Lake Lebarge
    I cremated Sam McGee.

—*Robert W. Service*

REQUEST FOR REQUIEMS

Play the *St. Louis Blues*
For me when I die.
I want some fine music
Up there in the sky.

Sing the *St. James Infirmary*
When you let me down—
Cause there ain't a good man
Like me left around.

—Langston Hughes

A SILLY YOUNG FELLOW NAMED HYDE

A silly young fellow named Hyde
In a funeral procession was spied;
  When asked, "Who is dead?"
  He giggled and said,
"I don't know; I just came for the ride."

—Author Unknown

Angels Sing-a-Ling-a-Ling

For me the angels sing-a-ling-a-ling
They've got the goods for me.
—AUTHOR UNKNOWN

THE CRUSADER

Arrived in Heaven, when his sands were run,
   He seized a quill, and sat him down to tell
The local press that something should be done
   About that noisy nuisance, Gabriel.

—Dorothy Parker

JOSHUA HIGHT

Beneath this plain pine board is lying
   The body of Joshua Hight,
"Cheer up," the parson told him, dying,
   "Your future's very bright."

Slowly the sick man raised his head,
   His weeping friends amazing.
"Parson, it's most too bright," he said,
   "For I can see it blazing!"

—Author Unknown

ON A PURITANICALL LOCK-SMITH

A zealous Lock-Smith dyed of late,
And did arrive at heaven gate,
He stood without and would not knocke,
Because he meant to picke the locke.

—*William Camden*

FOR A LADY I KNOW

She even thinks that up in heaven
    Her class lies late and snores,
While poor black cherubs rise at seven
    To do celestial chores.

—*Countee Cullen*

FOR A MOUTHY WOMAN

God and the devil still are wrangling
    Which should have her, which repel.
God wants no discord in His heaven;
    Satan has enough in hell.

—*Countee Cullen*

A CURT ADDENDUM

A Cape Cod widow who had not got on too well with her late husband objected to the stock verse which was chiseled upon his stone.

As I am now so you will be,
Prepare for death and follow me.

She went out one dark night and scratched beneath it:

To follow you I'll not consent
Because I know which way you went.

—*Author Unknown*

EPITAPH FOR ANY NEW YORKER

I, who all my life had hurried,
    Came to Peter's crowded gate,
And, as usual, was worried,
    Fearing that I might be late.
So, when I began to jostle
    (I forgot that I was dead)
Patient smiled the old Apostle:
    "Take your Eternity," he said.

—*Christopher Morley*

151

Grave Humor

Quiet is requested for benefit of those who have retired.

—AUTHOR UNKNOWN

EPITAPH FOR A POSTAL CLERK

Here lies, neatly wrapped in sod,
Henry Hankins c/o God.
On the day of Resurrection,
may be opened for inspection.

—*X. J. Kennedy*

ON A POLITICIAN

Here, richly, with ridiculous display,
The Politician's corpse was laid away.
While all of his acquaintance sneered and slanged,
I wept; for I had longed to see him hanged.

—*Hilaire Belloc*

from THE GREEK ANTHOLOGY

I saw no doctor, but, feeling queer inside,
Just thought of one—and naturally died.

—*Translated by Humbert Wolfe*

JOHN COIL

Here lies John Coil,
A son of toil,
Who died on Arizona soil.
He was a man of considerable vim
But this here air was too hot for him.

—Author Unknown

HERE LIES MY WIFE

Here lies my wife: here let her lie!
Now she's at rest——and so am I.

—John Dryden

DUST TO DUST

After such years of dissension and strife,
Some wonder that Peter should weep for his wife;
But his tears on her grave are nothing surprising—
He's laying her dust, for fear of its rising.

—Thomas Hood

156

EPITAPH ON JOHN KNOTT

Here lies John Knott:
His father was Knott before him,
He lived Knott, died Knott,
Yet underneath this stone doth lie
Knott christened, Knott begot,
And here he lies and still is Knott.

—Author Unknown

ON SAMUEL PEASE

Under this sod and beneath these trees
Lies all that's left of Samuel Pease.
Pease ain't here,
It's just his pod;
He shelled out his soul
Which flew to God.

—Author Unknown

WITHIN THIS GRAVE DO LIE

Within this grave do lie,
Back to back, my wife and I;
When the last trump the air shall fill,
If she gets up, I'll just lie still.

—Author Unknown

THIS SPOT

This spot is the sweetest I've seen in my life,
For it raises my flowers and covers my wife.

—Author Unknown

STRANGER CALL THIS NOT

Stranger call this not
A place of gloom;
To me it is a pleasant spot—
My husband's tomb.

—Author Unknown

GRIEVE NOT FOR ME

WOMAN:

> Grieve not for me my husband dear,
> I am not dead but sleeping here;
> With patience wait, prepare to die,
> And, in a short time, you'll come to I.

MAN:

> I am not grieved my dearest wife,
> Sleep on, I've got another wife.
> Therefore I cannot come to thee
> For I must go and live with she!

—Author Unknown

ON AN OLD TOPER BURIED IN DURHAM CHURCHYARD, ENGLAND

Beneath these stones repose the bones
  Of Theodosius Grimm,
He took his beer from year to year,
  And then his bier took him.

—Author Unknown

THOUGHTS FOR ST. STEPHEN

Instead of the Puritans landing on Plymouth Rock
(Said Jo Davidson, the delightful sculptor)
How much pleasanter this country would have been
If Plymouth Rock
Had landed on the Puritans.

—Christopher Morley

EPITAPH ON THE PROOFREADER OF THE ENCYCLOPEDIA BRITANNICA

Majestic tomes, you are the tomb
Of Aristides Edward Bloom,
Who labored, from the world aloof,
In reading every page of proof.

From A to And, from Aus to Bis
Enthusiasm still was his;
From Cal to Cha, from Cha to Con
His soft-lead pencil still went on.

But reaching volume Fra to Gib,
He knew at length that he was sib
To Satan; and he sold his soul
To reach the section Pay to Pol.

Then Pol to Ree, and Shu to Sub
He staggered on, and sought a pub.
And just completing Vet to Zym,
The motor hearse came round for him.

He perished, obstinately brave:
They laid the Index on his grave.

—Christopher Morley

A SERIO-COMIC ELEGY
Whately on Buckland

In his "Common-Place Book," Archbishop Whately records the following elegy on the geologist Dr. Buckland:

Where shall we our great professor inter,
    That in peace may rest his bones?
If we hew him a rocky sepulchre
    He'll rise and break the stones,
And examine each stratum which lies around,
For he's quite in his element underground.

If with mattock and spade his body we lay
    In the common alluvial soil,
He'll start up and snatch these tools away
    Of his own geological toil;
In a stratum so young the professor disdains
That embedded should lie his organic remains.

Then exposed to the drip of some case-hardening spring,
    His carcase let stalactite cover,
And to Oxford the petrified sage let us bring,
    When he is encrusted all over;
There, 'mid mammoths and crocodiles, high on a shelf,
Let him stand as a monument raised to himself.

—Archbishop Whately

ST. SWITHIN

"Bury me," the bishop said,
"Close to my geranium bed;
Lay me near the gentle birch.
It is lonely in the church,
And its vaults are damp and chill!
Noble men sleep there, but still
House me in the friendly grass!
Let linnets sing my mass!"

Dying Swithin had his whim
And the green sod covered him.
Then what holy celebrations
And what rapturous adorations,
Joy no worldly pen may paint——
Swithin had been made a saint!

Yet the monks forgot that he
Craved for blossom, bird and bee,
And, communing round his tomb,
Vowed its narrow earthen room
Was unworthy one whose star
Shone in Peter's calendar.

"Who," they asked, "when we are gone
Will protect this sacred lawn?
What if time's irreverent gust

Should disperse his holy dust?"
Troubled by a blackbird's whistle,
Vexed by an invading thistle,
They resolved to move his bones
To the chaste cathedral stones.
But the clouds grew black and thick
When they lifted spade and pick,
And they feared that they had blundered
By the way it poured and thundered.
Quoth the abbot: "Thus, I deem,
Swithin shows us we blaspheme!
He was fond of wind and rain;
Let him in their clasp remain!"
Forty days the heavens wept,
But St. Swithin smiled and slept.

—*Daniel Henderson*

OUTSIDE THE CHANCEL DOOR

Here I lie outside the chancel door,
Here I lie because I'm poor.
The further in the more they pay
But here I lie as warm as they.

—*Life*

WANG PENG'S RECOMMENDATION
FOR IMPROVING THE PEOPLE

Having read the inscriptions
Upon the tombstones
Of the Great and the Little Cemeteries
Wang Peng advised the Emperor
To kill all the living
And resurrect the dead.

—*Paul Eldridge*

Index of Authors

Index of Titles

Index of First Lines

About the Compilers

Mrs. Brewton was born in Americus, Georgia, and was graduated from the State Normal School in Athens, Georgia. Dr. Brewton was born in Brewton, Alabama; he was graduated from Howard College in Birmingham, and received his M.A. and Ph.D. from George Peabody College for Teachers in Nashville, Tennessee. He has also done graduate work at Columbia University. He is now Professor Emeritus of English at George Peabody College for Teachers.

Dr. and Mrs. Brewton have compiled a number of anthologies of poetry and verse for children, and Dr. Brewton has written many articles on education and children's literature.

The Brewtons are folklore enthusiasts, and they both enjoy gardening in their spare time.

About the Illustrator

Ellen Raskin is a well-known illustrator and author of children's books. She has received awards for her work from the Art Directors' Club of New York, the Society of Illustrators, and the American Institute of Graphic Arts.

Miss Raskin was born in Milwaukee, Wisconsin, and majored in art at the University of Wisconsin. She enjoys music and composes songs for the harpsichord and piano. She lives in New York City with her husband, Dennis Flanagan, and her daughter, Susan.